The Great Depression

by Michael Burgan

Content Adviser: Professor Sherry L. Field,
Department of Social Science Education, College of Education,
The University of Georgia

Reading Adviser: Dr. Linda D. Labbo,
Department of Reading Education, College of Education,
The University of Georgia

COMPASS POINT BOOKS

Minneapolis, Minnesota

Compass Point Books
3722 West 50th Street, #115
Minneapolis, MN 55410

Visit Compass Point Books on the Internet at *www.compasspointbooks.com* or e-mail your request
to *custserv@compasspointbooks.com*

Photographs ©: Hulton Getty/Archive Photos, cover, 10, 12, 21, 26, 33; Library of Congress, 4, 8,
31, 32, 34, 37; Franklin D. Roosevelt Library, 5, 22, 24, 25, 40; Stock Montage, 6, 7, 9, 13, 14,
17, 27, 28, 30, 38, 39 (all); The Mariner's Museum/Corbis, 15; Bettmann/Corbis, 19.

Editors: E. Russell Primm, Emily J. Dolbear, and Deborah Cannarella
Photo Researcher: Svetlana Zhurkina
Photo Selector: Linda S. Koutris
Designer: Bradfordesign, Inc.
Cartographer: XNR Productions, Inc.

Library of Congress Cataloging-in-Publication Data
Burgan, Michael.
    The Great Depression / by Michael Burgan.
       p. cm. — (We the people)
    Includes index.
    ISBN 0-7565-0152-0 (lib. bdg.)
       1. United States—History—1933–1945—Juvenile literature. 2. United States—History—
1919–1933—Juvenile literature. 3. Depressions—1929—United States—Juvenile literature.
4. New Deal, 1933–1939—Personal narratives—Juvenile literature. 5. United States—Economic
conditions—1918–1945—Juvenile literature. [1. Depressions—1929.] I. Title. II. We the people
(Compass Point Books)
    E806 .B915 2002
    973.917—dc21   2001001589

TABLE OF CONTENTS

AMERICA HITS BOTTOM

The United States had gone through bad times before, but Americans had never seen anything like the winter of 1932–1933. Millions of workers had lost their jobs and many had also lost their savings when local banks closed for good. Some parents searched through garbage cans hoping to find food for their children, while homeless people lived in shacks made of cardboard and scraps of wood.

During the Great Depression, food and shelter were often hard to come by.

Franklin D. Roosevelt's radio broadcasts helped Americans begin to feel more confident that their situation would eventually improve.

Poverty and despair marked the first years of what is now called the Great Depression. The slump that started in 1929 was the worst in the nation's history. During the 1930s, the economy improved slightly. President Franklin D. Roosevelt brought a confident attitude and new ideas to Washington, D.C. But the depression worsened again in 1938 and did not end until the United States entered World War II in 1941. The Great Depression and the nation's response to it changed forever how the U.S. government worked, and what it would do to help the poor.

THE ROARING TWENTIES

The dark years of the Great Depression seemed impossible just a few years earlier. For many Americans, the 1920s were the "Roaring Twenties." Productivity boomed—factories needed fewer workers to make more goods. Workers made higher salaries than they did before World War I (1914–1918), so they could afford to buy cars and new products such as radios and refrigerators. People who could not afford to pay for an item simply bought it on credit. They took home a radio or a car and made a small payment on it each month.

During the 1920s, Americans were able to afford more products that made life easier.

Save time, energy and money
—don't market every day

The General Electric Refrigerator is unusually roomy and it keeps all food healthfully fresh

Republican Calvin Coolidge, president of the United States from 1923 to 1929, believed that "the business of America is business." He and his advisers said companies and the rich should be free to do as they pleased. The government should not get involved in the economy, and everyone should have a chance to make a

President Calvin Coolidge

fortune. For many, the stock market was the way to do this.

Companies sell shares of stock as a way to raise money. The stockholders are the owners of the company. Based on how many shares they own, they receive a share of the money the company makes. During the 1920s, millions of new investors joined the stock market. Stock prices rose, and the investors thought they would keep going up. People who didn't have enough money borrowed the cash to buy stocks. They believed they would quickly make enough money to pay off the loan.

DARK SIDE OF THE BOOM

These good times hid some of the problems that were already cropping up. Higher productivity meant that some people could not find factory jobs—machines now did the work they once had done. Unemployment in industries such as coal mining and textiles soared during the 1920s. Farmers also faced hard times. The prices for food fell, but the farmers kept growing crops and raising livestock. Soon farmers could not earn enough money to live on.

Farmers had a particularly difficult time during the Great Depression.

8

America faced another damaging trend during the 1920s. Wealth was not equally distributed among all its citizens. By 1929, the richest 24,000 families in the nation owned 34 percent of all the money saved in America. About 21 million families had no money saved. In business, companies made higher profits, thanks to rising productivity. But they did not often pass on these profits to their workers by paying higher salaries.

Over time, fewer Americans could afford to buy the goods coming out of U.S. factories but the companies kept

U.S. companies were making more goods than Americans could buy.

9

The poor and unemployed often received food from charity soup kitchens.

on producing the goods. This was called under-consumption, and it further weakened the economy. The problem was global too. World War I left many Europeans in dreadful poverty, so they could not afford to buy U.S. goods either.

For the most part, poor and unemployed Americans could expect no help from the federal government. President Coolidge and other leaders believed the government should not help people during hard times. They believed that private groups should give charity, not government officials in Washington.

BLACK THURSDAY

The cracks in the U.S. economy widened during 1929. Too many people were borrowing too much money to buy stocks. This worried the Federal Reserve, a part of the government that controls the supply of money. The agency tried to slow the borrowing by making it more expensive for banks to lend money. At the same time, more companies were struggling to stay in business. Construction projects were decreasing, and the problems in farming worsened.

A giant jolt to the U.S. economy came on Thursday, October 24, 1929, when the price of stocks began to tumble. Shareholders rushed to sell their stocks before the prices fell even further. Soon panic gripped New York's Wall Street, the home of the most important U.S. stock exchange. That day became known as "Black Thursday." One journalist wrote, "The excitement and sense of danger which imbued Wall Street was like that which grips men on a sinking ship."

11

Crowds gathered on Wall Street in New York City the day the stock market crashed.

Leading bankers quickly pledged to spend millions of dollars to help raise stock prices. The move fell short. After Black Thursday came Black Tuesday—October 29th—when stocks dropped about $14 billion in value. Just seven weeks earlier, the stock market had reached an all-time high. Now, many small investors saw their wealth wiped out.

12

Stocks dropped about $14 billion in value on Black Tuesday.

FROM BAD TO WORSE

Despite the crash in stock prices, some government and business leaders did not worry. Herbert Hoover, another Republican, was now president. Immediately after the crash, Hoover assured Americans that "the fundamental business of the country . . . is on a sound and prosperous course."

President Herbert Hoover

Like Coolidge, Hoover did not want the government to get overly involved in the economy. However, he differed from Coolidge in other ways. Hoover said the government had a role to play in the economy in some cases. Unfortunately, one action he took actually made the situation worse.

Foreign goods, such as these bananas, were taxed more heavily.

In 1930, Hoover approved the Smoot-Hawley
tariff—a tax on imported products. Hoover hoped this
tax would stop Americans from buying foreign goods
and convince them to buy more U.S. goods. But most

15

Americans lacked the money to buy *any* goods at all, not just imported goods. Also, European countries responded by taxing U.S products, which hurt the sale of American goods in Europe.

Hoover took other steps. He asked business leaders not to cut wages. He also asked the Federal Reserve to lower the interest rates they charged on loans. He wanted people to have more money to spend. Hoover was trying to boost the people's confidence. If people think the economy is slowing down, they are reluctant to spend money. Their lack of spending then hurts the economy even more.

Hoover called this difficult time a "depression." He thought this word seemed less harsh than "panic" or "crisis," words used to describe earlier business slumps. By the middle of 1930, President Herbert Hoover told Americans his policies were ending the depression. "We have now passed the worst," he said, "and . . . shall rapidly recover."

Instead, the Great Depression worsened. More businesses closed down and the ones that survived made less

Banks across the United States failed and closed.

money. More banks shut down too. Their customers,
like many stockholders during the stock market crash
of October 1929, saw their life savings disappear.

17

NEW EFFORTS

Hoover realized that the federal government had to do more. At his request, Congress created the Reconstruction Finance Corporation (RFC). This agency loaned money to banks and insurance companies to help them stay in business. Another government program provided money to banks that made housing loans.

Despite these efforts though, many Americans sought stronger government action. Senator Robert La Follette Jr., a Democrat, wanted to give direct aid to the unemployed. By 1932, 12 million people were out of work. La Follette said Hoover "lacked either the understanding or the courage to . . . **alleviate** the distress of the unemployed and . . . reduc[e] the number out of work."

Hoover clung to his belief that the government should not give "charity" to the poor. He wanted local and state officials to help the unemployed. But these officials could not take care of everyone.

Senator Robert La Follette Jr.

THE BONUS ARMY

In 1932, some people warned that the United States was facing a disaster. Americans who lacked jobs, food, and housing were becoming desperate. A newspaper editor who toured the country told Congress, "I do not say we are going to have a revolution on our hands within the next year or two . . . but the danger is here."

Violence did break out in July. Thousands of World War I veterans and their families marched to Washington, D.C., demanding early payment of benefits they were supposed to receive in 1945. About 2,000 of these people set up a campsite and refused to leave the city. They became known as the "Bonus Army." General Douglas MacArthur, acting on his own, ordered armed soldiers to drive the Bonus Army out of Washington. A journalist described the scene: "The cavalry clattered down Pennsylvania Avenue with drawn sabers. The infantry came marching along with fixed bayonets." The soldiers

World War I veterans camped out in front of the U.S. Capitol.

used tear gas on the veterans and burned down their campsite.

The attack on the Bonus Army seemed to represent the government's attitude. Many Americans thought Hoover did not care enough about the poor. When the presidential election was held in November, voters rejected Hoover and elected Franklin D. Roosevelt (FDR).

FDR

At that time, Roosevelt was governor of New York. He came from a wealthy family and was related to former president Theodore Roosevelt. FDR used a wheelchair.

One of the few photos showing FDR in a wheelchair

He had lost the use of his legs after contracting polio in 1921. Some people thought this physical challenge helped Roosevelt understand the suffering of others. His physical problem also seemed to shape his confident attitude. "If you had spent two years in bed trying to wiggle your toes," Roosevelt said, "after that anything would seem easy."

Voters liked Roosevelt's upbeat approach. During the 1932 election, Roosevelt talked about a "New Deal." His government would help the poor and pull America out of the Great Depression. At the time, however, no one— including Roosevelt—knew exactly what the New Deal would be.

When Roosevelt was sworn in as president on March 4, 1933, he told Americans, "The only thing we have to fear is fear itself." Roosevelt called on many experts to help with the New Deal. They were known as his "Brains Trust." The president also relied on his wife, Eleanor. The First Lady shared FDR's concern for the victims of the Great Depression, and she helped win support for the New Deal.

Franklin Delano Roosevelt was sworn in as the 32nd president on March 4, 1933.

To get out his message, Roosevelt often spoke on the radio. Millions of Americans heard these "Fireside Chats," making Roosevelt the first president to use radio in an effective way.

24

THE FIRST NEW DEAL

Almost immediately, Roosevelt called Congress to meet. This session began what is now called the "Hundred Days." Roosevelt also declared a national bank holiday to try to help banks stay in business. The banks closed for four days, so that savers could not pull out their money. Then Congress created the Federal Deposit Insurance

President Roosevelt declared a bank holiday to help stop the runs on the nation's banks.

25

Corporation (FDIC), a new agency that guaranteed savers would not lose their money if a bank failed. That ended the rush to pull savings out of banks.

During the Hundred Days, the government created many new programs and agencies. The Agricultural Adjustment Administration helped farmers. The National Recovery Administration (NRA) asked businesses to guarantee certain wages and cut working hours. And for the

The Civilian Conservation Corps hired young men to work in the nation's parks and forests.

first time, the federal government gave direct aid to the states to help support the poor. Later the government began creating jobs programs for the unemployed. The Civilian Conservation Corps hired young men to work in the nation's parks and forests.

Another successful New Deal agency was the Tennessee Valley Authority (TVA). The government built dams along a series of rivers that run through seven southern

The TVA was another federal project designed to end the depression.

27

Providing work for the unemployed was one of Roosevelt's priorities during the depression.

states. The TVA dams provided electricity and helped control flooding. The entire TVA project pumped billions of dollars into the region.

Roosevelt tried many ideas to help the poor but not

28

all of his plans worked as he had hoped. Slowly, however, more people went back to work, though unemployment was still high. One young man in Rhode Island told a government official, "I've been looking for a job for four years. . . . There's nothing for us!" In 1934, Roosevelt told the nation that relieving suffering was still his most important goal. "In a land of vast resources," he said, "no one should be permitted to starve."

Not all Americans wanted the government so involved in the economy. Some business owners and wealthy people accused FDR of limiting their freedom. These people preferred the policies of Coolidge and Hoover. FDR's critics said the president wanted socialism. Under socialism, the government owns and runs many businesses. Roosevelt said he simply wanted to save the U.S. economic system of capitalism, not replace it with socialism. Still, the president's most bitter foes even refused to call him by name. He was simply "that man in the White House."

THE SECOND NEW DEAL

In 1935, Roosevelt introduced a new series of programs designed to combat the Great Depression. These programs were later called the Second New Deal and some historians say they were even more important than the First New Deal.

The WPA helped build roads, airports, and parks.

A poster publicizing the new Social Security program

One part of the Second New Deal was the Works Progress Administration (WPA), later known as the Works Projects Administration. Over several years, the WPA hired more than 8 million Americans. The WPA built roads, bridges, parks, and airports. The WPA also hired artists. Some produced plays; others created paintings and sculptures for public buildings.

Another new program was Social Security. This insurance program helped the unemployed, the elderly,

The African-American community strongly supported FDR during the 1936 election.

and the disabled. Some critics said Social Security did not go far enough to help the poor but once again the idea showed Roosevelt's desire to get the government involved in the economy.

Roosevelt easily won reelection in 1936. Most Americans accepted his New Deal. He drew support from many groups including immigrants and their children, factory workers, city residents, and African-Americans. This "New Deal **coalition**" became the heart of the Democratic Party for years to come.

CONCERNS AND CONFLICTS

Many Americans, however, still had problems. In the Great
Plains, severe drought and bad farming methods had
created a "Dust Bowl." Huge dust storms covered the
region with thick, black dust. "Everything was full of dust,"
said one Oklahoma resident. "You'd end up with dust in
your food and you'd feel it in your teeth." Many farmers
went to California, looking for jobs that often did not exist.

The effects of the Dust Bowl devastated American farmers.

The Great Depression was particularly devastating to African-Americans.

African-Americans also suffered. They had higher unemployment rates than whites did, and their living conditions were often worse. Because of discrimination, many New Deal programs were not carried out fairly. African-Americans did not always get the help they deserved.

Workers also struggled. They won the right to form unions, but many companies resisted them. Unions gave workers the power to demand better wages and working conditions. Companies and unions often battled over these demands. Many workers went on strike, refusing to do their jobs until their demands were met. These strikes sometimes led to violence.

Roosevelt also caused trouble for himself with a plan to add members to the U.S. Supreme Court. The court had struck down some of Roosevelt's New Deal programs, including the NRA. He hoped to add new judges who would not challenge his actions. Even Roosevelt's supporters attacked this plan to "pack" the court with judges who favored the New Deal.

Unemployment rate 1929–1939
15%–25%
Over 25%

CANADA

Washington
Oregon
Idaho
Montana
N. Dak.
Minn.
S. Dak.
Wisconsin
Wyoming
Nevada
Utah
Colorado
Nebraska
Iowa
California
Arizona
New Mexico
Oklahoma
Kansas
Missouri
Illinois
Ind.
Ohio
Kentucky
Tennessee
Arkansas
Texas
Louisiana
Miss.
Alabama
Georgia
Florida
Pennsylvania
New York
Maine
Vt.
N.H.
Mass.
R.I.
Conn.
New Jersey
Md.
Del.
W. Va
Virginia
North Carolina
South Carolina

Dust Bowl

Pacific Ocean
Atlantic Ocean
Gulf of Mexico
MEXICO
N

0 200 miles
0 200 kilometers

A map showing the U.S. unemployment rate from 1929 to 1939.

BAD TIMES AGAIN

Another problem hit Roosevelt in 1937. The president's new programs had cost billions of dollars. Roosevelt thought they were working so well that he could now cut government spending. The cuts, however, led to a mini-depression called a recession. By March 1938, almost 4 million more people

Once again in 1938, unemployment in the United States rose.

Benito Mussolini

were unemployed. This time, however, Congress quickly called for new spending to provide aid.

In 1939, more than 9 million Americans were still out of work. While relief programs lessened some of their problems, the Great Depression was still all too real. Many of these people did not go back to work until the country prepared for war.

During the 1930s, tensions had risen in Europe. In Germany, a Nazi **dictator** named Adolf Hitler was in power. Another dictator, Benito Mussolini, controlled Italy. And in Asia, Japan had invaded China. As Roosevelt and his advisers focused more on world events, the country began to spend more on defense, preparing for a possible war. Even this spending did not put everyone back to work, however. Only America's entry into World War II in 1941 truly ended the Great Depression.

"All the News That's Fit to Print."

The New York Times.

Copyright, 1939, by The New York Times Company.

EXTRA

VOL. LXXXVIII...No. 29,806.

NEW YORK, FRIDAY, SEPTEMBER 1, 1939.

THREE CENTS

GERMAN ARMY ATTACKS POLAND; CITIES BOMBED, PORT BLOCKADED; DANZIG IS ACCEPTED INTO REICH

BRITISH MOBILIZING

Navy Raised to Its Full Strength, Army and Air Reserves Called Up

PARLIAMENT IS CONVOKED

Midnight Meeting Is Held by Ministers—Negotiations Admitted Failure

Bulletins on Europe's Conflict

London Hours of Warsaw Bombing

French Confirm Beginning of War

Attack on Entire Front Reported

First Wounded Brought Into Gleiwitz

HOSTILITIES BEGUN

Warsaw Reports German Offensive Moving on Three Objectives

ROOSEVELT WARNS NAVY

Also Notifies Army Leaders of Warfare—Envoys Tell of Bombing of 4 Cities

FREE CITY IS SEIZED

Forster Notifies Hitler of Order Putting Danzig Into the Reich

ACCEPTED BY CHANCELLOR

Poles Ready, Made Their Preparations After Hostilities Appeared Inevitable

Hitler Acts Against Poland

HITLER GIVES WORD

In a Proclamation He Accuses Warsaw of Appeal to Arms

FOREIGNERS ARE WARNED

They Remain in Poland at Own Risk—Nazis to Shoot at Any Planes Flying Over Reich

Hitler Tells the Reichstag 'Bomb Will Be Met by Bomb'

Chancellor Vows 'Fight Until Resolution' Against Poland—Gives Order of Succession As Goering, Hess, Then Senate to Choose

German dictator Adolf Hitler attacked Poland and war spread across Europe.

RESULTS OF THE GREAT DEPRESSION

The Great Depression hit millions of Americans with brutal force. The bad times made many people question

Before the Great Depression, private charities supported the poor or unemployed.

American values. Before the 1929 stock market crash, most people accepted the ideas of Coolidge and Hoover. They agreed that America was a country of individuals who should be free to make all the money they could, and that help for the poor should come from private groups, and not from the government. FDR and his New Deal created a new set of values and ideas: the government should sometimes hold back business and take an active role in helping the poor. Today, many politicians try to balance and blend these two sets of beliefs.

The New Deal created a larger and more effective federal government. This government still cannot prevent depressions or recessions. But the Great Depression showed that the government could—and should—ease the worst suffering of the poor and the unemployed during hard times.

GLOSSARY

alleviate—lessen

coalition—union; alliance

dictator—a ruler who takes complete control of a country, often unjustly

tariff—a tax that raises the price of imported goods

DID YOU KNOW?

- Franklin Delano Roosevelt was the only U.S. president to be elected to four terms of office.

- From 1933 to 1942, more than 3 million young men enrolled in the Civilian Conservation Corps. They each earned $30 a month.

- The Works Progress Administration supported thousands of artists who created 2,556 murals and 17,744 pieces of sculpture that decorate public buildings all over the United States.

IMPORTANT DATES

Timeline

1929	Herbert Hoover takes office as president. The U.S. stock market crashes, plunging into the Great Depression.
1932	Franklin D. Roosevelt defeats Hoover in the presidential election.
1933	Roosevelt declares a bank holiday and begins his New Deal programs.
1935	Congress passes Social Security, the most important feature of the Second New Deal.
1936	FDR easily wins reelection.
1937	U.S. economy begins to slide into a recession.
1938	Congress approves aid for the unemployed.
1939	World War II begins in Europe.
1940	FDR wins reelection again, becoming the first president to serve three terms.
1941	United States enters World War II.

IMPORTANT PEOPLE

CALVIN COOLIDGE

(1872–1933), *thirtieth president of the United States; was in office during the "Roaring Twenties," just prior to the Great Depression*

HERBERT HOOVER

(1874–1964), *thirty-first president of the United States; in office when the Great Depression began*

ROBERT LA FOLLETTE JR.

(1895–1953), *Wisconsin senator who was critical of the Hoover administration*

DOUGLAS MACARTHUR

(1880–1964), *U.S. general who drove the Bonus Army out of Washington, D.C.*

ELEANOR ROOSEVELT

(1884–1962), *wife of Franklin Delano Roosevelt; supported social programs and humanitarian causes*

FRANKLIN DELANO ROOSEVELT

(1882–1945), *thirty-second president of the United States; guided the country through the Great Depression*

WANT TO KNOW MORE?

At the Library

Joseph, Paul. *Franklin Delano Roosevelt*. Edina, Minn.: Abdo & Daughters, 2000.

Nishi, Dennis. *Life During the Great Depression*. San Diego: Lucent Books, 1998.

Ross, Stewart. *Causes and Consequences of the Great Depression*. Austin, Tex.: Raintree/Steck-Vaughn, 1998.

On the Web

The American Experience—The Presidents: FDR

http://www.pbs.org/wgbh/amex/presidents/nf/featured/fdr/fdec.html

For biographical information about Franklin Delano Roosevelt

Herbert Hoover Presidential Library and Museum

http://www.hoover.nara.gov

For a virtual tour of the Hoover library

The New Deal Network

http://newdeal.feri.org

Includes photographs and articles about the Great Depression

Through the Mail

Center for New Deal Studies

Roosevelt University

430 South Michigan Avenue

Chicago, IL 60605

For publications about FDR and his New Deal administration

On the Road

The Museum of the Franklin D. Roosevelt Library

4079 Albany Road

Hyde Park, NY 12538

800/337-8474

845/229-8114

To visit the Roosevelt home and learn more about the lives of Franklin and
Eleanor Roosevelt

INDEX

About the Author

Michael Burgan is a freelance writer of books for children and adults. A history graduate of the University of Connecticut, he has written more than thirty fiction and nonfiction children's books for various publishers. For adult audiences, he has written news articles, essays, and plays. Michael Burgan is a recipient of an Edpress Award and belongs to the Society of Children's Book Writers and Illustrators.